On A

ZIG ZAG

TRAIL

The Flow of Life

J. J. BHATT

1

ISBN: 9798644724536

Title:

On A Zig Zag Trail

Author:

J.J. Bhatt

Published and Distributed by Amazon and Kindle worldwide.

This book is manufactured in the Unites States of America.

PREFACE

ON A ZIG ZAG TRAIL: The Flow of Life is a tale of humanity's constant struggle while walking through the road of uncertainty and many twists and turns. The Zig is compassion, courage and hope whereas the Zag offers dark side governed by the seven sins. Throughout the historic time, humans have preferred to follow the 'Middle Way' of the trail, but that is inadequate today. Specifically, the Middle Way of life has given humanity nothing but the Pandora's box full of deadly nukes, growing dangers of climate change and recurring threats of killer germs: Ebola, Spar, Corona and still unknown numbers of their cousins to pop-up either intentionally or accidently!

Today humanity enjoys unprecedented material comforts and the techno dependency on one hand and continues to suffer from fear and anxiety on the other. It is therefore a necessity we the twenty-first century citizens must seek new ways of adapting global cooperative attitude to design a viable vision which would lean more toward the Zig side; allowing it to be a dominant force over the old destructive habits of the Zag . Once such a goal as alluded is accomplished, would be possible to begin the purpose-driven journey not just to live, but to live well on this astoundingly beautiful Planet Blue!

On A Zig Zag Trail along with my previous titles, I have attempted to present the poetic expressions akin to highly energetic world famous falls: the vibrant Niagara, majestic Iguassu and the magnificent Victoria. These inspiring falls as stated have always fascinated me since childhood, whence sharing my thoughts in this special way with the world.

J.J. BHATT

CONTENTS

Preface 3
Zig Zag Trail............9
Future is Now......... 10
Universal speak.......11
Passage..................12
Human Will........... 13
Life 14
Intention 15
Last Sight............. 16
Caveat.....................17
Design................... 18
Pulse.................... 19
Verdict 20
Unity 21
Maroon... 22
Illumination.......... 23
Sweet Hymn 24
Precocious............ 25
Flow of Life......... 26
Irony of Fate....... 27
Lighthouse.......... 2 8
Our Time 29
Affirmation .... .30
Gratitude 31
My soul............. 32
Swirling 33
Gantelet 34
In Essence 35
Locked-up....... .. 36
Gusto.............. . . 37
Be Human........ 38
Measure........... .39
Get This.............40
New Path........... 41
Young Blood......42

A Point of...............43
Continuums 44
Payback............... 45
Empty.................. 46
Juxtaposition......... 47
Middle Way......... .48
Light & Shadow.... 49
Real Self.............50
Pivot 51
The 50th 52
Confession 53
That's It.............. 54
Think................... .55
Dream Girl 56
Gardner.............. .57
Insidious 58
Honesty............... . 59
Fragility.............. .. 60
Tango Magic........ 61
New Beginning...... 62
History Sings........ . 63
Ultimate.... .... .64
Sanguine 65
Existence 66
Catharsis 67
Puzzle....................68
Milieu................... .69
Journeye...............70
Flash................. ... 71
That's Us............... 72
Watch Out............. 73
Sacred Fire........... 74
Purifier...................75
Expedition 76
Good Morning........77

Pretender..............78
Be Smart..............79
Be alert................ 80
Ripple Effect...... ..81
New Direct.......... 82
The Flow............ 83
Shadows............. 84
Perfunctory..........85
Tears................... 86
Single Track....... 87
Pursuit................ 88
Misfired............. 89
Flow of Life.......90
Upwells............. 91
Tall Human........92
Revelation 93
Precious Gift...... 94
Fate................... 95
Magic 96
Self-Reliance.....97
Achilles'............ 98
Tragedy............. 99
Confession....... 100
Spineless.......... 101
Awakened........ .102
Killer Bees....... 103
In Sync......... .. 104
Equalizer 105
Beware............106
Clarity 107
Delusion......... ..108
The Spin...........109
Wrong Way......110
Lady T..............111
Breakout...........112
Our Story......... 113
Go Beyond...... 114

Moral Will.....................115
Newspeak 116
Twists & Turns.............. 117
Today Matters................118
Convergence................ 119
Explorers..................... 120
Grandeur.................. ...121
Vision Upward............. 122
Janus City...................123
The Voice.................. 124
Eternity.................. .. 125
Purification...................126
Dear Lady................. 127
Think! 128
Love........................... 129
Mettle..........................130
Thunder................. 131
Venus 132
Determined................. 133
Lady Love.................. 134.
Future Ringing.......... 135
A Note 136
Motif........................... 137
Spark........................... 138
Riddle .... .139
Sisyphus.................. 140
First Step..................... 141
Escape.................... 142
Hope Unto Life...... 143
Resilience................ 144
Location.................. 145
Stirs........................... 146
Let's roll......................147
Salute.................... ...148
Last Word............... . .149
Reality.................... 150
Recurrences................. 151

Reminder..................... 152
Winner....................... 153
Double-Decker 154
Dilemma.................... 155
Bridges Only.............. 156
Coiled Spring 157
Subjectivity................ 158
Never forget.............. 159
Publications............. . 160

Zig Zag Trail

Humans
Keeps walking
Through the
Zig Zag trail
Yet
Doesn't know
Way to their
Destiny so well

As a child,
Enjoyed playful
Days and slowly
Kept soaking
Life's experience
As much as
They can

On maturing,
Rejected all what
They learned and
Sought to
Correct their
Imperfect world

They're now
Determined to
Write a new story
Of the
World once again...

Future is
NOW

We've
Turned
Materialistic,
Hedonistic and
Techno cursed
Damnable beings,
Of course

Seems
We're
Hanging onto
Insecurity and
Fear alright

But we
Don't want
To let go the
Old
Habits anymore

AI's
Shall legally
Steal many million
Jobs and in return
Real humans
Shall get few bucks
Merely to exists...

Universal-
Speak

I've
Already
Expressed
My dream
Many times
Before

But now
Let my
Soul speak
In silence
Instead

Though
I've
Evolved
Through my
Blessed time;
Don't know
How far yet
To go...

Passage

Death
What may be
A blinding light
Showing the way
To eternity or what

It
Patiently
Waits for every
Blessed soul
To pay the toll
For a birth

Death
What a
Meaningful
Closer to life
As it
Purifies every
Soul
Never before...

Human
Will

**Human
Will
What a
Magical force
To know
*All That Is***

**It's
The power
Behind
All my moral
Missions**

**It's
The inner
Strength of
My spirit to
Spill over
Million dreams**

**It's the
Thread that
Ties together
All lose ends
To give meaning
To my existence...**

Life

Life
Where
Blessed world is
In constant turmoil
Where evil and
Chaos keeps defining
The exotic ambience

The
Challenge
Always keeps
Knocking our
Conscience and
We don't
Care to respond

What's
The point
In engrossing
Nostalgic
Remembrances
Of the past

When
Future is asking
To get ready and
Face the issues of
Of our time...

Intention

Ahh
The spirit
Always
Pointing upward
To make me
The hero of my
Own time

What a
Fascinating
Experience it is
While
Rolling toward
The realm of
Perfection

How far
Do I
Keep going
Before
I meet my
Waiting dream...

Last
Sight

Last
Sight of
My sibling
Who was nobly
Laid on a blazing
Funeral pyre

Last
Touch of
Love
I ever felt when
I closed his eyes

Last
I ever prayed
Was his
Grand journey
To eternity

Crackling flames
From the fire brought
The message from him,
"Brother don't tear
For 'am on my way
To a happy place
Where
I shall meet you
One day again..."

Caveat

Wonder
If judgment of
Life is
About behavior,
Ethics and belief

In that case
Why
Haven't we
Exercised 'em
Consistently to
Be meaningful
Beings

For any
"Moral war
Within"
There is a
Possibility of
Misjudgment

In other
Words,
There is a
Moral limit
While walking
Through
The Middle Way
Of our
Zig Zag Trail!

Great
Design

So long
We think we're
Better than others,
And so long
We keep imposing
Our will on others
We remain
Shackled by our
Miserable
Short comings

Sadly,
We shall continue to
Suffer through the
Waiting blank pages of
History yet to be inked

What's
The point in
Mourning when our
Collective moral sense,
Reason and right vision
Have turned into
A propitiating
Sacrifice!

Pulse

We've
Heard of
Recurring
Apologies,
Guilt's
And grief's

And we
Wonder
Why bad
Happens to
Good folks
Now and then

Is there
Something
Missing from the
Human equation
Or what

We've
Sailed
Through many
Stormy Seas and
Never afraid
Still
We wonder,
"Why something
Still missing from
Our total experience?

Verdict

What if
Death purifies
The corrupt spirit

What
If life
Gives chance
To write the
Story again

And what if
Life says:

Try to
Clarify the
Meaning and
Spare me from
Your worries

Well to that,
Death
Laughingly
Replies:

Individual life
Shall turn into
An urn,
But the cycles of
Life and death
Shall spin forever!

Unity

Let
Power of
Our will be
The chariot
Riding through
The violent
Battlefield

From birth to
Death
The battles on
And unity of our
Spirit be the
Force that we
Must never quit

At this
Time
Firmness of
Courage must
Take charge and

Let the
Determined will
Be the
Golden chariot
Riding through
The violent
Battlefield...

Maroon

When
A human
Feels stranger
In his home
Marks a great
Tragedy, indeed

His dream
Seemed shattered
Into million
Pieces of despair
And dark days
Engulfs him
Everyday

He's
Disillusioned
By the reality
He's in and
Keeps thinking
To end his life

Human,
What a
Good intention
Lost in the hellish
Sphere of
Anxiety and fear...

Illumination

Being
A child of
Zillion stars
He keeps on
Shinning so well
With wit and
Curiosity to know
This vast Universe

Yes,
Human's willing
To chase freedom
Even he has to
Soar high above
Worldly limits

Let
Enlightenment
Be his first
Bold step

Let the
Star child
Understand
His inner Self
While in this vast
Universe...

Sweet
Hymn

As I strive
To be above
The cloudy
Grey skies

I soar
Higher and
Even higher as if
'Am a free bird

Yes,
'Am ready to go
Beyond false piety,
Pseudo claims and
Imposed restraints
On my freewill

Let
My spirit keep
Soaring higher and
Higher from this
Time on to sing:

What
A sweet
Shinning hymn
Of a dream
Taking me toward
Infinite possibilities
Of my own being...

Precocious

What
Wonderful
Children we're of
This grand
Mother Universe

We
Keep happily
Singing her
Beauty but
Not knowing the
Lyrics so well

We
Children are
Always in a hurry
We think
We're creator of
Our reality but
Fail to know
What's the goal
Of our being in it

No doubt,
We are
Cosmic seeds but
We should never
Forget
We're mortals and
At times
Damn fools too!

Flow of Life

When
Death is
Silently calling
To enter the
Gateway to
The unknown
Place

That's when
Human arrives in
His full senses and
Ask, "why didn't
I balance my
Insight in time"

When life
Collides with death
Only few awakened
Souls welcome it
With calm

For them
Life was always
A positive force
That gave chance
To say,
"Goodbye with
A big smile..."

Irony of Fate

While
Reading
The history
One realizes,
Human is saga of
Two opposites:

Rational- emotional
Moral- immoral and
Good –evil and so on

What a far cry
From the dream of
"Human perfection"

Thanks
For holding
Onto
The old habits:
Ignorance,
Arrogance and
Indifferent attitude

All adding to the
Tribal madness
Powered by
Myriad myopia,
Phobia and no
Sophia!

Lighthouse

Under the
Shadows of
The Lighthouse,
Islanders kept
Watching the
Oncoming nasty
Waves eroding
Their dreams

Foggy
Night after night
Limited their vision
To grasp clarity of
Their fate

They thought
Lighthouse was
The best venue to
See far toward the
Inspiring Sea

Well
To their chagrin
They can't see
Farther anymore
While
Caught into
The unforgiving
Foggy scene...

Our
Time

**Why not
Point upward
Far above the
Miserable state
We've been in
For a very long**

**Don't let
Greed and
Self-interest
Keep us in this
Cage too long**

**Time to
Transcend
The old Divine
And probe beyond**

**Time to
Demand
Our privacy,
Dignity and
Freedom
Here and now...**

Affirmation

Before
Death calls
We got to choose
How to
Reach the Temple
Of good intention

No reason
To be dwelling
With evil
Inclination

No reason
To stick with
A false belief
That burdens
The free spirit

Before
It's too late,
Let's take a bold
Stand to defend
What is right?

Yes, what's
Right for the
Moral value
Every time...

Gratitude

Let us roll
A red carpet
To the heroes
Who've inspired
Us for a long

Let us
Open hearts
To those lovers
Who've stood tall
Through chaos of
Their romance

Let us
Remember on
This day of
July 4th those
Fallen heroes

Who
Gave their
Precious lives
So we can enjoy
Freedom day after
Day for a long...

Human
Soul

I am a singer
Going town to town
To let my lyrics run
Through the hearts of
Millions young around
The world

I am a poet
Going from mind
To mind to let 'em
Know the world
Around 'em is
Nothing but
Beauty and truth

I am a painter
I roll out a giant
Portrait of
Human nature
Stretched between
Known to unknown

I am
An ordinary
Spirit still trying to
Know where 'am
Heading
Either here or
To eternity still
Don't know so well...

Swirling
Winds

**Life
What a
Recurring
Melody of
Trials and errors**

**At times,
Man may think,
"It must be a terrible
Blunder to be here?"**

**He even
Tried different
Brands of worships
To resolve his
Puzzling questions**

**Why is
He still
Fears to lose
All his material
Comforts**

**Wonder,
Why is he
Caught by the
Swirling winds of
Uncertainty of
His worship!**

Gauntlet

Let the
Star child
Wake-up

Let him
Be
The creator
Of
His noble
Mission

Let him
Bring forth
His humanity
To the surface

Let him
Pick up the
Gauntlet

Let him
Try to be
Human-divine
Again!

In
Essence

Fanning
Flames of
Million errors
Burying
Him under a
Thick pile of
Misjudgments

First
Was the
Egregious
Claim of many
Brands of God

Second,
That curse of his
Irrational belief
To crush others
For insane reason

Third,
Falling into
The abyss of
Greed while
Destroying
His moral being...

Locked-up

When
Strolling
Through a
Busy boulevard
In any big city

I see
Folks keep
Walking with
Heads down while
Talking through
Their tiny e-toys

They keep
Walking but
Ignoring
Traffics and
Often get hit by
Equally crazy
Driver who's
Also busy with
His dear e-toy

When
Strolling
Through a busy
Megacity,
Modern humans
Not the same
As we knew 'em
Once before!

Gusto

Life
Full of vigor
Rollicking with
Cheerful rhythms
Melodies and lyrics

And there is
The golden Sun
Striking all souls
To keep shinning
In the name of
Their truth

Life
Asking to
Keep the
Journey going
Yes urging
To keep singing:

To grow,
To grow and
To grow with
Wisdom,
Love and hope

That's
Where
He's his own
Truth that he
Must know...

It's Time

Modern
Human
Suffering
From
Crazy whims as he
Fails to know his
Moral being

Modern
Human
Turning into
An insecured
State of mind

He's
Concerned
With super smart
AI's imposing long
Term consequences

That's
Where he's
Locked-in and
Asking
To save his
Soul!

Measure

Man is
A measure of
Understanding
And deep insight of
His life and time

He's also
An owner of
His birth and
Deliverance of
Hope and peace

He's an
Inspiration to
Young braves
If he strengthens
His moral will

Human
What a treasure
Troll of potential
Yet to prove his
Worthiness...

Get
This

It seems
We enjoy life
Half and half

Half
With good
And half with
Not so good

In such a
Mixed up scenario
We're suspended
Between hope and
Despair and

We're never
The same as we keep
Growing up with right
And wrong

O the patterns of
"Middle way existence"
Bringing nothing but
More chaos and disorder,
Violence and war...

New
Path

Let's
Begin our
Long walk
Along
The unity of
Collective
Intention

It's time to
Back-off from
Mythic illusion
And let
Our vision be
Driven by the
Rational thought

Time
To seek
Harmony
To reach our
Collective dream
Of peace and joy...

Young
Blood

Yes
We're young
Braves who're
At the helm from
This point on

It is
Clear
We've won some
We've lost few but
We've balanced
'Em well
Time after time

We've
Loved with
Sincerity
We've lost in
Agony and
We've balanced
'Em well

We've faced
Challenges
Time after time
But we've
Shown our best
Each time...

A
Point of
View

It's
One big
Nada if
We abuse
Glory of
God to pursue
Our selfish
Ambitions
Behind the
Closed doors

It's
One big
Betrayal
If we
Don't know
How to
Steer the
Space ship
Through the
Prevailing
Challenges of
Our time...

Continuum

Life ain't
A beginning
But a continuum
Experience

Death ain't
Capitulation
Albeit its
A triumph over
One more cycle
Of existence

We're
Tested in many
Ways while
In suspension
Between
Life and death

In life
We must awaken
Our inner strengths

It's before
Death we must
Boldly declare:
"I did it my best way"

Pay Back

They cried,
"Redemption"
But the
Deaf world
Didn't hear
Their call
So well

Well
The saga
Continues to
Be written in
In red ink

Good men and
Women
Caught into
Head-winds of
A corrupt world

They're
Demanding
Freedom
In the name of
Harmony and Peace
With a noble intent...

Empty
Shell

All is
Transitory
And inadequate
In the big picture
Of reality

But
Human seems
Not to care for
Consequences of
His misdeed

Armed with
Such attitude and
Heavy burden of
Selfish need
He
Doesn't care but
Willing to carry
Ton of greed for
No good end...

Juxtaposition

Though
God is immortal
But
No match to
Human mortal

Though
Almighty resides
In His heavenly
Bliss and never
Suffers cruelty or
Habit of greed;
Mortals do

While God
Offers belief and
Divine command
It's human who
Endures through
Hardship of
Trials and errors
Of existence

Oh yes,
God may be the
Conceptual thought
Who's eternal but
Human who is a
Reality ending always
In his supreme death!

Middle Way

Piety and
Passion what an
Explosive cocktail
Mix

Piety
Peddles duty,
Devotion and
Pious pomp

Passion
Dances with
Emotional
Intensity of anger,
Lust, grief and fear

Is human
Ready to pay
The price of
Right and wrong
As he keeps
Walking through
Golden path of
The Middle Way!

Light & Shadow

Often
I wonder
Who's better?
Is human over
His dear Divine,
Or what!

Well
Lord dwells
In the heavenly
Bliss
While human caught
Into the world of
Constant conflicts

Human
What a dynamic
Evolving thinking
Machine
Always powered
By his
Determined will

Dear Lord
Is at sleep in
His heavenly bliss
While human
Keeps struggling
For his durable
Peace...

Real

It's not so
Relevant where
'Am I today or
Where was I
Yesterday

Let me
Just look
Ahead and
Know my way

Let
My will take
Me out of the
Cacophony of
All 'nay Sayers'

It's
Not relevant
What I think or
What I do everyday
It's
How I bring forth
Moral worth in this
Human form has
Significance to
My existence...

Pivot

What if
These
Intricacies of
Relationship
Fading so quick

If we
Miss this
Golden opp
We may not
Swim anymore

Let's
Not sorrow
Over our
Misdeeds

Let's
Learn to
Give a
Meaning to
Our
Noble births...

The 50th

Today
We're in the
Right place and
Don't wish to go
Back
Where we're
Before

Since
I found
Her
Fifty fabulous
Years flew
By so soon

Call it
Our luck,
Call it whatever
Is steady alright

Life
What a
Marvelous surprise
Always revealing
Meaning after long
Struggles and few
Triumphs of course...

Confession

When fate
Keeps titling
Toward
Dark days

Man ask,
"How long
Must he
Walking for
Better days?"

All along
He thought
He was the owner
Of his destiny

Now
Seems it was
One big
Optical illusion

Being
Though
Disappointed
Fails to reckon
He's been pushed
All along a
Wrong track...

That Is

In
The end,
Only
Moral souls
Shall survive
For they have
A purpose to
Prevail

Let no
Man be
Prisoner in
The cavern
Too long

Let no
Woman be
Victim in the
Male-dominant
Realm anymore

Let's ask,
"Why rot in
The world of turmoil
When peace is waiting
So long!"

Think

Don't
Reject the
Spiritual
That's
Where
We are
Originals

Don't
Dance with
Evil
It shall
Kill our dream

Don't
Run away
From
Troubles but
Face 'em instead

Let's roar
Before
The deaf world
With one voice:
Be fearless
For that's
Who we are!

Dream
Girl

She's
Perfect
In shape
And form

She's
A beauty,
Slim and tall

She's
Majestic
And
Fearless
Indeed

Damn right
She's
A lovely
Girl and
She's
A sharp knife
As well!

Gardner

Let the
Gardner
Grow hope,
Love and joy
For she's the
Real hero,
Par excellence

Let her
Balance the
Motley garden
Into art of
Her good

Let her
Inspire all
Young hearts
To save
Such a
Garden of
Beauty & truth...

Insidious

At times,
Love
Blasts like a
Dynamite and
It's called,
"Betrayal"

And there's
Nothing left, but
The shattered
Dreams which
Can't be pieced
Again

Love
What an
Explosive human
Experience

Remember,
Caesar and
Antonio got
Sucked into
Cleopatra's
Seductive
Arms

Love what a
Fiery passion
What a
Hypnotic spell
That can't be tamed
If laced with lust
And greed...

Honesty Knocking

After
Taking a
Close look
At existence
Truth
Must emerge:

We're
Corrupt
Social animals
Chasing after
Our individual
Selfish wish and
Not for
Good of the whole

Let's
Not pretend
Let's
Not get upset
Let's
Face our truth
And begin to
Rethink what
We must be at this
Time...

Fragility

You never
Know
Where you're
Heading while
Walking through
The Zig-Zag trail

You never
Know
Where you
May be
When trying to
Enter
The high society

You never
Know
Where you're
Going when
You're the
Accidental death
On the zig zag trail,
Already!

Tango
Magic

It was a
Tango Night
We're young
And curious to
Know new mate

Once
Music began
We forgot
Formalities and
Were lost in our
Sweet dreams
Alright

It was a
Fiery tango
That captured
Our throbbing
Hearts at once

No
Questions asked,
'Til dawn broke
The long silence

We
Hugged and
Exclaimed:
What a beautiful
Experience it was
Between
Two loving souls!

New Beginning

A couple
Packed-up all
Their possessions
In dozen boxes and
Hopped onto their
Old van

Yes, they're
Leaving the town
Where they lived most
Of their time

Oh yes,
It was a mixed
Feelings to leave
Million memories
Behind, but the future
Was so tempting to
Ignore

As they drove off
Familiar landmarks,
They cheered and said,
"Goodbye old struggles
And pains... time to enjoy
New dreams from this
Point on..."

History
Sings

Causation
Must be indeed
A priori maxim
That's where the
Divinely seed is
Sowed

As it began
To grow in
Human Mind
Slowly robbed
His free will
Through time

Well,
Pious servants,
And zealots alike
Took over the
Sacred machine

And began
Drumming-up
Their special
Brand of Divine

Consequence,
The world got
Nothing but
Myopia, phobia and
Bloodshed in return...

Ultimate

All is
Passing by
In different
Shapes and forms
Depicting a journey
From unity to
Complexity in fact

Either it's
A metaphysical
Insight or an
Empirical query
Must
Converge to know
The truth behind

Let him
Move from
Self –centered to
Selflessness
From self-love
To love of humanity
If he desired to
Meet his noble goal...

Sanguine

Her life is
Filled with
Love, intrigue
And
Challenge
Within

Where
Real
Meaning of
Her
Existence
Must be
Revealed

Let her
Leave
Footprints of
Her courage

Let her
Inspire
Young to
Rewrite
Their own story
In return ...

Existence

**Human
Surely
A warrior of
Survival**

**He
Gets up to regain
Inner strength to
Survive day by day
Simply**

**He's caught
Between
His inner being and
Good Lord but
Chooses to remain
Silent for some odd
Reason**

**He knows
Life ain't fair to
Ordinary like him
And accepts the
Battle must go on
'Til the victory is
His final reward...**

Catharsis

Why let
Tears and
Remorse's
Keep slamming
His daily dreams

Man
Got no where
To go but to
Fight for a
Just cause

As he
Gathers-up
His determination
He must roar wild:

"Why
Be afraid of
Terror,
Ignorance and
Humiliation
When I'm
The sole force of
My every good."

A Puzzle

We
Hold life so
Dearly for us
Only

Why
Not the same
For fellow
Billon beings!

In
Misery and
Pain
We're unity
Over and again

Why
Then in joy
We go our
Separate ways!

Milieu

Battered by
Constant
Barrage of
False values
Of the time

Humans
Fallen so weak
To exercise
Their freewill's

"Beware, Beware"

Shouted the man
Of wisdom in a busy
Supermall,

"Humanity
Is slowly
Descending
Into its
Apocalyptic end"

Sadly,
Most folks
Passed through
While Ignoring
The wise man...

Journey

Love
What a deep
Experience
To cherish

No
It's not the
Ordinary love
We know so well

Its
The special
Love
That evolves
From
Self-love to the
Universal love

To arrive
At such a lofty
State of feeling
Demands a
Disciplined
State of mind

It also ask
To defeat the
Seven deadly sins
Before getting on
Its right track...

Flash!

**Why
Human is
Nonchalant
To know his
Own essence**

**Wonder
Why is he
Profusely
Ambiguous
To grasp true
Meaning of
Existence**

**Is it
Lack of deep
Insight or is it
His negligence
Not to know the
Truth at all!**

We are

We're the
Universal theme,
Eternal hope
And never-ending
Fear
At the same time

We've
Read stories of
Life and death
Through symbols
And metaphors
Now and then

We've
Been always
In self-love and
Unable to meet
The final goal

And we
Keep asking,
"Why, why...why
Me?" when misery
Strikes at the core...

Watch
Out!

**After
Having
Betrayed
Loyal friends**

**Man atlast
Came to senses,
He had been a
Liar and a social
Foe for a long**

**Guilt etched
His soul so deep
Yet he continued
To pretend being
Superior
Than others**

**Human
Nature
What a
Stubborn
Arrogance and
Greed always...**

Sacred Fire

No, no don't
Get me wrong
"Am   your pal
Came to let you
Know we're
To begin a new
Daring journey
Together at
This very time

Dear lady,
'Am here to rinse
Off all our sins:
Be calm and
Let the light of
Our strong bond
Get us through
This stygian night"

After a pause,
Fire turned into
Human form and
She knew he was
Her life-soul as
Listened:

Yes dear lady
Today is the test of our
Vows ...it's the fire of our
Love, our love...our love
That is all...that is all so
I welcome you to my world
This is far away from
Life we shared once before...

Purifier

Man
What a perpetual
Thinker full of
Insatiable desire to
Know his Self

Much of his life
Passed by so quick
While pursuing
Selfish big goals

In his youth
He witnessed ugly
Wars, bunch of lies
And learned how to
Gain power, money and
Fame

At the height of
His success
Suddenly
He lost interests
For egotistic goals
And emerged as a
Total free spirit

In his final
Moment he said,
"Life seemed absurd,
But death is serene
That's why I leave
With no regrets, but
Peace of my soul"

Expedition

Folks on an
Expedition
Going nowhere
But circling the
Old habit of
Tribal fever
Alright

What a
Heavy burden
To carry- on
What a
Great stress
To bear

Let young
Launch a new
Expedition
With neither
Constraint nor
Any guilt at all

Let 'em be
Free from the
Blunders of their
Elders today...

Good Morning!

We've
Slumbered
For a long
While the
World kept
Spinning faster
Than we can
Reckon

Time to
Cast off
Petty pride,
Show-offs and
Come back to
The waiting
New Day

Time to
Wake-up
To new way
Of greeting
One another
With respect
And big smile...

Pretenders

In the
Milieu of
High
Societal elites

There
Often harbors
Lies, deceptions
And envy but
In a very refined
Ways, of course

Folks
Up over there
Dwell in the
Opulent palatial
Ambience and
Always so
Comfy but
Far from the
Reality of
Struggles and
Pains of many

Surely
Though they
Got tons of money
Yet they're equal
In mortality with
Billion others indeed

Be
Smart

Don't let
Evil breed evil
That's the direct
Passage to hell

Don't
Turn the
Story of guilt's
And regrets
That's the
Ignominious
Defeat alright

Don't fall
Victim to
One tragedy
After another
That's not the
Reason we're
Here and now

Don't
Sell soul
For hedonistic
Lifestyle
That's the
Immoral way to be
A techno slave indeed...

Be
Alert

If we
Slumber
Too long
We shall be
Doomed
Before asking,
"What
Happened?"

It
May be too
Late
To get off the
Shackles of
Our misdeeds

Only
An instant of
Awakening shall
Shall help us face
The challenge
Head-on...

Ripple Effect

War
What a dark
Necessity!

War
What insanity
To begin with

War
What an asinne
Way to pile up
Million dead

War
What a
Blatant sin

War
What a
Tragedy of
Intelligent beings!

New
Direction

We
Got no clue
What's our
Correct role
To heal the
Troubled world
Today

Let
The fog vanish
And let
Clarity of truth
Awaken our thick
Heads

Let young
Take charge of the
Uneasy state of
Present existence

And
Let elders
Go home and repent
For their collective
Misdeeds...

The
Flow

In
Totality
Of all
That is alive

Death is
Final and
Irrevocable
Indeed and

There is
No
Great riddle
Left behind

Only
Life makes
Sense
That's why
It is the
Last chance

Life
Where
We can be reborn
With a new name:
Hope
Harmony and joy...

Shadows

When
Caught by the
World of
Subjectivity of
Right and wrong

Truth
Hardly remains
Pure and
Never so simple
To grasp

In such
Shadows of grey,
Only
Moral ambiguity
Stand as one big
Constant

And there
Erupts a
Conflict
Between artistic
Sympathy and
Ethical judgment

And we don't
Know so well
Who's right and
Who's not in such
Shadows of the grey...

Uncertain World

All I know
Is the
World keeps
Evolving
With no
One direction

It's a
Roller coaster
Bringing new in
And exiting old
In an instant

Natures
Furies, wars
Or the germs
Upsetting the
Balance of life
Greater than ever

In
Such a fragile
World of
"Comings and goings"
Humanity remains
In the throes of
Death always...

Tears

To die
Into the
Cold hands of
Guilt
Must be the
Worse legacy
A man can leave
Behind

To betray
Trust of a
Good friend
Must be the
Worse sin
A man can ask
Children to
Remember

Failing to
Forgive the
Innocent
Who's
Begging with
True tears
Must be the
Worse blunder
A man can leave
Behind...

Single
Track

Myths,
Worships,
Arts, music or
Right or wrong
Beliefs
Kept humans going
Since the very
Beginning

Proving
Beings are
Seeded in the
Archetype of
The collective
Unconscious

Which
Gave 'em
Strength to keep
Spinning over and
Again through the
Zig Zag trail and
Still not reaching
The final goal...

Pursuit

Didn't we
Try
Many times
To understand:
Death is
Irrevocable and
There ain't
An escape!

Didn't we
Try
Many times
To understand:
Why
Human remains
Imperfect and
Almighty
So perfect

Didn't we
Try
Many times
To understand:
Reason
Opens
The world of
Awakening
In the end!

Misfired
Missile

During the
Course of his noble
Journey
A good man with
Simplistic attitude
Got tangled into
The seductive world of
Money, fame and lust
To feel
So good of course

Instantly, he turns
Into a complex greedy
Living machine; losing
Appetite for all that was
Honest and good before

He's
Now a new man
With a disgenous
Smile and very
Hungry to be
Far richer than
What he's been

In the end,
He can't fulfill his
Insatiable addiction
And finds his salvation
Through untimely suicide
In his lonely room!

Flow of Life

Life
Bound up with
Death is like
Two lovers lost
In the storm of
Ecstasy and pain

When
Human is
Caught
In the middle of
Two opposing
Forces

Nights
Turn into
Nightmares and
There is no solace
To hang on

In such
A state of stress
His very being
Begins to
Obliterate into
A meaningless
Existence, *que vie*

Upwells

It's
In existence
Where challenges
Pop-up now and
Then

It's
In mind
Where conflicts
Arise and die
On their own

It's
In the heart
Where friction
Can eventually
Kill love

It's
In memory
Where
Million regrets
Stirs up instantly...

Tall
Human

Mortals
Keep
Walking through
The trail that is
Not straight but
Zig and zag
In its basic design

It's the
Night that gives
Him rest as well
Fear to think

It's the
Killer storm
Threatens all his
Big dreams

Rain or shine
Mustn't he
Determined
To be reborn
Larger than life?

Revelation

When
Chaos turns
Into clarity and
Hate into love

It's
A sobering
Experience to
Soothe the soul

What
An amazing
Thought to
Unite
Humanity,
At last

Let's
Be aware
We're all
Equal in
Deep spirit and
Of course
In death as well...

Precious
Gift

Each
Got the wish
Something
Worth to be

Yet,
Each in
Collision with
Wisdom within

Each
A precious
Gift born to be
Harmony and
Peace

Yet,
Each in
Collision with
Greed within

Human
What a story
Of constant
Contradictions
And conflicts...

Fate

She was a
Bad memory
Who
Kept embattling
With new vigor
Every time

Once
A beautiful
Quiet and dignified
Princess of
Royal etiquette

And many suitors
Were ready to extend
Their hands, but she
Couldn't find the one
She could love

And, there landed a
Young handsome brave
Who captured her heart
But he wasn't royal kind
For that he was killed by
Imperial power in charge

That's the way
The world of status,
Wealth and power
At times operates
Even today and it's
A sad story alright...

Magic Hope

Beyond
Cynism and
Despair
We got to stick with
Hope and nothing
But hope

For hope is a
Floating survival
Kit keeps
Us from drowning
Into
The Dark Sea of
No return

Let us be
Preponderant
Force of
Our positivity

Let us
Get off our
Self-centered
False piety

Let us
Face life
With a sense of
Gratitude and
Magic of hope
Simply...

Self-Reliance

Human
What a sum
Total of all
Experiences and
Be the owner of
The right direction
To head-on

Don't
Let him shake
His head in
Disbelief and
Lot of doubts

Don't
Let him
Question
His inner being
Today or at
Any time soon...

.

Achilles
Heels

When
They eat many
Exotic animals
Without a hygienic
Sense
No wonder why
Deadly microbes
Threatened
Whole humankind
And
That's the first sin

For allowing
Only one nation
To be the
Single mega-factory
Of the world
That's the second
Sin

When
Reasonable
Profit turns
Into
An irrational
Greed that's
The third sin...

Tragedy

As history
Moves on so does
Humans with their
Determined will
To make it through
Alright

As
Petty religious
Doctrines keeps
Breeding ignorance,
There goes also
Erosion of
Spiritual unity
In return

Let
Noble humans
Show their courage
To bring unity,
Peace and dignity,
Instead...

Confession

Let's
Not be afraid
To grasp the
Magnitude of our
Collective reality
Today

Let's
Be honest
To confess
We're
One imperfect
Humanity since
The beginning

We're
Not yet at
The Temple of
Perfection but
Must band together
To reach over there
On time

Let the
Zig Zag Trail
Be the
Straight arrow
To get us to
The Temple of
Our truth...

Spineless

Why
Guardians are
Failing to attain
Right vision and
Peace!

Why not
Demand our
Collective moral
Strength in this
Twenty-One

When
Shall we
Verily realize
History is a
Repeating
Blunders every
Now and then

Why
Not prepare
Our collective
Ethical will at this
Calling time...

Awakened

Yes,
Mortals
Who we are
Born to be
Greater than
Our deaths

Mortals
We're keeping
Rolling along
Our big dreams

Mortals
Who we're
Still searching
The totality of
Our meaning

Mortals
Who we're
To know well
We're never far
From our deaths...

Killer
Bees

Every
Human begins
Life with an
Equal
Innocence and
Infinite curiosity
To know the world
So well

During
Childhood
If they encounter
Deceptive learning;
Blatantly sowing seed
Of violence in their
Tender heads;
Turning 'em into
"No-think killer
Beings"

A hellish day
Arrives on the
Scene

When
They surface as
Bigots, zealots
And idiots
Inflicting
Their senseless
Dark sins...

In Sync

We're no
Longer sovereign,
If we fail to grasp
What's
The meaning of
Our justification
To be humans

We're no
Longer sovereign
If we fail to
Bring young braves
Into the fold to join
The noble mission

We're no
Longer sovereign
If we fail to acquire
Social moral sense
With a spirit of
Well-being of the
World

Not God but
Our rational
Supremacy and
Sheer endeavor of
Goodwill shall
Free us in the end...

Equalizer

Unity of
Purpose is a
Very fragile
State of mind

A slightest
Doubt or a
Tiniest wrong
Can upset its
Scale in no time

Let the
Call for unity
Be gentle and
Sincere in its
Intention

Unity is most
Effective when
Human species
Faces fear of
Mass extinction

What a funny
Situation:
Unity
Emerges only
From common fear
Of survival but
Not from our
Collective goodwill!

Beware

It's
A sad saga
When a person is
Reduced to nothing
But a few ounces of
Urn

In due
Time he/she
Shall be forgotten
And no memory
To recall

It's
A sad saga
When a person's
Dignity is stolen and
Reduced to nothing
But to a ton of dirt

It's
A sad saga
When ignorance
Sets the fire of
Hatred and wars
Reducing
Humankind into
Moral nothing...

Clarity

While
Holding on to
His final breath
A man recollects
His time on earth

Once
He looked
Reality from a
Different point of
View

He thought
He had grasped,
Nothing but
The fragility of
Existence in
Total sense

He concluded his
Life though bobbed
Up and down in the
Sea of the seven sins,
He kept swimming
Against all odds
To make it through

And still
He was happy to give
A big smile as he waived,
Goodbye to the world
Where he struggled but
Equally loved so much...

Delusion

**What if
Super intelligent
Creatures monitored
Us from a far away
Place and may say:**

*Look at these tiny
Worms with big egos
Dwelling on an
Insignificant grain
In this vast cosmos*

*Why do they
Keep judging
In the name of their
Divided abstruse God
To soothe their guilty
Souls always*

*Why these
Petite rascals, yes
These imperfect souls
Keeps running here
And over there for
Nothing in the end*

*Just look at their
Sanctimonious
Self-chosen servants
Who keeps barking but
Not with reason at all...*

The Spin

Life often
Blends itself
In weird ways:

Hedonism
And morality
Good and evil
Right and wrong
And all rolls on
Simultaneously
Through nice
And easy,
"The Middle
Way"

Life often
Swings between
Grief and joy,
Love and hate...
Us and them and
Nothing good comes
Out of such milieu
Of the Middle Way

The mental spin
Keeps alive
Romantic illusion,
Hypocrisy and fear
Time after time
Threatening
Freedom to survive...

Wrong Way!

As we
Pass
Through the
Muddy fields of
Anger, envy and
Tech highs

Collision is
Imminent
In our time

As we
Continue
To pass through
The false belief
Driven by greed

Collision is
Imminent
For bloody
Violence and war
And there should
Be no surprise!

Lady
Tragedia

They called her,
"A Pure Trouble"
To others she was
A one nasty
"Ms Manipulator"

Whatever may be
Her nick name
She was a romantic
Wanderer yearning
For her fantasies
Now and then

She didn't care
To be restrained
She didn't cared
Her vows
She was a wanderer
Night after night and
No humanity
In her heart

When
Her youth
Faded
Her fantasy
Took a nose-dive to
The world of regrets and
She never came back
To her common sense!

Break Out

Being
Stained with
Indignation, shallow
Talks and triviality
Of self-centered
Rewards

Brought to
Him nothing but
Disaster to the
Unity of his
Noble thought
He once held

Let' him go
Beyond barriers
Of million constraints
And let' him change
The course

Let him learn
To navigate in the
Right direction to
Meet the waiting
Goal...

Our
Story

Our story is
Evolved from
Ancient tales which
Is no different today
Than their time

Sometime
It's malevolent
And at times it's a
Saga of
Moral strength

Our story
Sometime so
Strange and at
Times friendly
To confess

Our glory
Sometime so
Stained and at
Times driven-by
Total ethical
Determination

Our story
What a flashing
Bolts of successes
And failures;
Upwelling from
The imperfect
Human thoughts...

To Go Beyond

On dying
We're liberated
From the shackles
Of our evil self

No wonder,
Why we look so
Tranquil in the
Final scene

As humans
We're ambiguous,
Driven by false tales
And that's the role
We play

Oh
Yes, we're
Prisoners caught into
The narrow circle of
Self-interests

No wonder
At the end of our
Journey
Why pious soul
Feels so free!

Moral
Will

Life
What a
Wonderful
Experience but
Sadly it's so brief

Human
What a
Sharpe vision
Yet unable to
Attain his
Noble dream

Why
Doesn't
He weaves
The fabric of
Past and present
With the needle
Of Moral Will!

Newspeak

The
Orwellian
World told
How to
Control human
Thought through
Manipulation of
Words

Dictators
Knew
The art so well,
To control the
Media and
In turn to
Control masses
Through their wills

In the
Process morality
Is deeply wounded:
Where
Slavery is called
Freedom and
Lie as make-belief
Truth

Hitler,
Mussolini,
Stalin...Mao and others
Played the old game but
They miserably failed
In the end...

Twists
& Turns

Life
Often gets
Tangled with
Facts and fictions
And at that point,
Reality turns into
One mighty mirage

It's as if
Humans lost their
Moral compass
And forgot where's
The right direction

Love too gets
Caught between
Infatuation and
Honest feelings and
I that case,
Romance turns into
One terrible mischief

When
Children
Are trapped
Into war zones
Their humanity
Dies before their
Time reaps to make
Positive difference
On their own...

Today
Matters

Man's been
Suffering
Since everything
Changes but
His very nature
At the core

In the
Twentieth,
Wars, violence's
And genocides
Revealed his dark
Side so well

In the
Twenty-first,
Techno-savvy
Humans riding
On the carousal
Of hedonistic
And no
Concern for the
Future consequence,
At all!

Convergence

There's
Always a renewal
Between forces
Of social cohesion
And
Individual liberty

We're born
To go through
The grind
Over and again;
Arriving
At a common
Point of awareness:

*Each
Is asked
To face his/her
Truth*

*Each is
Asked to know
His/her
Moral depth*

*Each is
Judged by
The measure of
His/her deed...*

Explorers

By
The strength
Of our
Intense will
We shall win,
I mean we shall
Win this game of
Riddles, enigmas
And puzzles with
Our own wits

No
Reason to
Hold back
No excuse
To back off
Let the
Bold journey
Continue on the
Zig Zag trail

Never forget
We're the theme
We're
The noble births
We're
The spirits of
Eternal Truth...

Grandeur

Think of
Designing a future
Where
Entire spectrum of
Existence
Turns into one
Worthy experience

Think
Singing a
Marvelous song
Where
Humanity is
Inspired to zenith

Think of
Children who
Are precious gift,
They're our hope,
Our harmony...our
Peace...our meaning
Indeed...

Vision
Upward

Let every
Child be the story
Of a big dream

Let every
Young Their
Reveal elders'
Hypocrisy and
Greed

Let 'em
Understand how
False belief and
Pseudo- tales
Messed up
Their world

Let 'em
Share
The story with
Billion others of
Their age

Let 'em
Lit the fire of
New awakening
In every soul today...

Janus City

Mega-city
Not a good place
For timid individuals
To be hanging around
For often they turn
Target of humiliation
As they fail to play the
Game

It's the
Megapolises
Which measures
Human worth
In terms of
Social status,
Wealth and fame

If they don't meet
Set criteria as said
They become instant
"Yes men"
Capitulating their
Dignity to new masters
Of the megacity

Once sucked into such
Seductive opulent milieu
Of megacity....only suicidal
Thought begins to revolve
To these helpless victims
What a tragedy of
Young good humans to
Go through such a hellish
Experience...

The Voice

Be it
A thinker,
An artist, a painter
Or a man with a
Common sense on
The street

Let 'em
Reinterpret
Life
From their
Own creative
Point of view

Let 'em
Streamline
Courage, unity and
Determined will
Through their own
Experience

Let 'em
Leave the
Cave by
Fulfilling their
Infinite possibilities
And creative will...

Eternity

This mighty
Notion of
Eternity,
The mother
Who
Keeps stealing
Time by the sec

Existence
What a
Tiny stretch
In the totality of
Dear Eternity

It's the
Metaphysical
Human spirit that
Transcends beyond
And lands into the lapse
Of Mother Eternity only

Eternity
What a very
Essence of human
Thinking
Where every soul
Reenters for a new
Beginning...

Purification

Soul
Purification
Been the
Recurring theme
For millennia

But the soul is
An implacable
Will albeit
An illumined spirit
Holding human
Conscience intact

Soul doesn't
Obey Mr. Death
Albeit
It's a string of
Fiery thoughts,
Freewill, compassion
Fearlessness and more...

Dear Lady

Dear lady
Full of beauty
In whom all my
Dreams
Been pouring
Since we began
Our journey

How do
I express my
Gratitude to her
Today, tomorrow
Or ever for giving
Love, laughter and
New life to me

Let me say,
Am the luckiest
To be with you
Through thick
And thin of our
Time

I lay
Red roses
Before this marble
To renew our
Old memories and
For showing me:

Why
Love can be a
Throbbing truth in
Humanity...

Think!

As we keep
Falling into the
Arms of romance
Let us be sure
That's the right
Descent

As we
Kiss for the first
Time in this lovely
Moonlit
Let us be sure
That's the right
Decision to enter
A new beginning

As we
Continue the
Bold journey
Let love be the
Power of our
Joint moral will...

Love

We shall
Endure through
Agony of love
Either in hell or
Heaven for sure

It doesn't
Matter
If we live or
Die but love
Shall live ever

Its
Love that
Brings life alive
While dancing
In her bosom

Lovers
May be mortal
But love remains a
Splendid Rose Garden
Season after season and
There's never
A complain but only
Beauty and truth...

Mettle

**Life
May fall apart
And dreams
May not
Materialized**

**In such a
Turmoil,
Misery and
Despair
May chisel off
Self-confidence**

**In
Such a bad
State of existence
Be sure to
Hold on to your
Courage**

**Don't
Let your
Moral compass
Down and
Don't let
Eternal hope
Disappear from
Your noble soul...**

Thunder

What
Unique
Experience for
Children of this
Magnifique
Young Universe,
Today

Let
'Em know
The value of
Moral strength
To beat any
Formidable foe
Anywhere in the
Young Universe

Let
'Em know
They got the
R ational Power to
Grasp truth of this
Magnifique young
Universe too!

Venus

The lady is
Beauty and
So deep in
Her feelings

She's got
The power
To turn
Dream into
Anything
She wishes

She is
Tender yet
She's
Unbeatable too

Don't ask
Her how to live
Don't ask her
To obey your will

If you
Care to be
Her lover
Listen to her
Every heart beat
And be sure to
Treat her good.

Determined
Will

Being at the
Pinnacle of life
Dancing with hope
And love as ever

He never quits
His goal
He never thinks
For himself
He's
A noble warrior
In real sense

Being
Ready
At the pinnacle
Of his
Rational thought
As he
Keeps dancing with
A single goal

He's
Never afraid
He never shies away
From erasing obsolete
Tribal mindset as well...

Lady
Love

Don't
Let him
Die
In despair

Just awaken
Him from his
Long slumber
And point
Right direction to
Roll

Don't
Let him dwell in
Misery and pain
Don't let him
Seek any excuse
To escape

Just
Illuminate
His mind and
Show him the
Way... how to be
A better man...

Future
Ringing

Bells of
History been
Ringing for a
While with
A grand roar:

God, Mercy
And His
Mighty Will

Sorry but the
Consequences
Didn't turn out
To be so mighty
In return

Time to
Grasp the power
Of human endeavor
Driven by
Rational and moral
Strengths

Its time
Let him reset the
Journey on his own
Along a right trail...

A
Note

Existence
Revolves with
Different point of
Views of
Many billion
Beings

Whence
Social conflicts
Ends mostly in
Subjective
Judgments

Where
Reason,
Compassion and
Compromise prevail
There is possibility of
Good life to live

Where
Barbarians
Prefers to settle the
Score with swords,
Guns and crazy whims
There is never a
Peace, hope or
Inspiration to save
The future of
Their kids...

Motif

Progress
Is an
Uneven path
For at every turn,
There is light and
Shadow all along

Progress
Converges
Good with evil
And human gets
Tangled into a
Confused
Spider web

Progress:
What a
Zig Zag trail
Filled with
Chaos, angst
And greed ...

Spark

Being
May not be
Esoteric
But got
The intuitive
Instinct
To know the
World he is in

He's
Indeed
The owner of
His potential
Full of infinite
Possibilities

Let him
Be free from
The burden of
False belief

Let him
Be a free spirit
To discover his
Noble worth...

Riddle

A man while confessing said,
"Father, in life I've been dying
Each day, but love has kept me
Going well"

"So what is your issue my son?"
Godly man gently asked
With an intrigue

"Well father, while I've faced
Both life and love in equal ways, why
Have I failed in my belief in God? "

"Son life and love are the gifts
Of the Almighty Divine
You mustn't confuse 'em"

"Father let me clarify
I 'm asking how do
I transform self-love to
The love of humanity"

"But that's humanism
And it's not godly thinking!"
Pious man defended his belief

"Thank you father for
Giving me your time"
Man left the little window
With many thoughts
Swirling around his
Three-pound machine...

Sisyphus

During the
Panoramic
Human history
Many billions
Walked
On this Earth

Each sought to
Know the meaning
Of existence but never
Got the right answer

They've been
Disillusioned
By the constant
Confusion and chaos
Yet they've stood the
Test of their times

Today
Many billions are
Also walking through
The same track and
Keeps embattling against
New challenges of nukes,
Cyber attacks and germs
And their bloody struggle
Never ends...

First Step

The
Goal of life
Is clear, but the
Message seems
Ambiguous
To begin with

Let's know
The mission is
Freedom, hope
And harmony in
The world

Alas
The message
Is lost ... thanks to
False narratives,
Pseudo godly claims
And stubbornness
To change for good

Let's learn
To shred-off
Old habits:
Envy, revenge,
Greed as the first
Step to be free...

Escape

**No point
In dividing
Humans
Into different
Camps for
It doesn't do
Any good**

**When
Existence is so
Temporal and not
So well understood
Collective pursuit
Can be very helpful**

**Let's
Escape from the
Deep hole of
Insecured feelings,
Violence and tribal
Illness...**

Hope
Unto Life

Contextual
Self
Explores
Infinite
Possibilities
From near and
Far beyond

Being
A life force;
Evolving from
Temporal to
The eternal yet
He doesn't
Know that yet

Yes, he's
Worthy of
Something
Much more
Than
His lingering
Illness of
Doubts and
Despairs...

Resilience

When
An individual
Is suddenly cut-off
From the pulses of
His humanity

He's
Forlorned,
Yes he's
Alienated
And for him
Life is simply
A meaningless
Enterprise

Let him
Know
Pains and
Struggles make
Each
Human stronger
Than before

Let him
Regain his will to live
Let him discover his
Own being before he
Quits the live scene...

Location

What if
We've entered
Into a dark cave
Where
No moral code
Exists

Will that
Kill
Our humanity
Or what

No matter
Wherever
We may be
Either in this
Smart Tech world
Or in the dark cave

There's
A danger of
Losing
Identity, privacy
And morality
In an instant!

Stirs

When
Irrational
Overwhelms
And destroys the
Spirit of humanity

Each human
Is forlorned
He's angry and
Suffers from a
Terrible anguish

In such
A miserable
State of high stress
He's ready to
Reject
All the wrongs of
His reality and
Seeks to
Redefine what life
Ought to be

That's been the
Spark of humanity
Triggered by a few
Great minds
Let's be
Inspired to be better
Than whom we are...

Let's Roll

Intelligent
Beings are
Here to begin
An enlightened
Civilization that shall
Last 'til the end of time

Let's
Roll up the sleeves
And get to work
For we haven't got
Generous time
To think

It's
Time to look
Beyond
Corruption, pollution
And the recurring
Killer germs

Time
To get off
The sewer pond and
Wash off our guilt's
And roll forward to
An Enlightened
New way of life...

Salute

We're the
Star-child
Roaming around
In this splendor of
Beauty and truth

We're the
Creators of our
Noble thoughts
To comprehend
What is
It all about

We're
Eternal reality
For we're fearless
Spirits never afraid
Either in life or
In death to meet
Our final mission...

Last
Word

Darling
Don't let me down
For 'am returning
Home soon

I mean,
Don't let me
Forget we've been
On this journey
For a long

Yes
Sweetheart
Ever since we met
Life's been sunny,
Smiling and so sweet

Please don't let
Me down for we're
The reality of our
Dream come true

I'll be back
Home as soon as
The insane war is
Over and

If I don't
Make it in case,
We shall meet in the
Same place next time...

Reality

It is
What it is

It is
What we think
It is

It is
Either real of
Unreal but all
It is

Ecstasy or
Agony
Its life what
It is

Being
What he's either
Life or death, but
That's he is

In the end,
It is all about
What ought
To be!

Recurrences

While
Walking
Through the
Zig-Zag trail

Wonder
If there's
A way
Transcending
Their cropped
Emotions and
Crocodile tears

They're
Asking to
Regain integrity
And
Moral earnestness
While walking
Through killing
Fields of the
Zig-Zag trail...

Reminder

Story of
Humanity
What a flow of
Life
That begins with
The birth, albeit
A first ray from
The rising Sun

It shines fully
Mid-day of adult
Years when all
Dreams must be
Fulfilled on time

In the
Golden years,
The Sun sinks into
Twilight and soon
Beneath the horizon
As human takes
His final bow

En route
Infinite furies and fires,
All shaping his destiny
And as the day ends so
Does his life but always
With his big grin...

Winner

**He's an
Insatiable spirit
And a perpetual
Curiosity
Always
Striving to
Reveal:**

*What's the
Meaning of
Being here and
Now*

**Human
What an
Incredible
Creative force
Ready to
Grasp his truth
In an instant...**

Double-Decker

We hear
By 2030 the world
Shall be a 'Double
Decker Bus'

At the lower level
Passengers shall
Ride free
That is, each will
Get salary for not
Working anymore!

At the top
Fewer super- smart
Thinking semi-humans
Shall call all the shots
And ride the bus with
Full control

Elites shall
Pay regular salary
To all leaders and
Their governments
In return,
They shall take
Orders from their
New masters

So foretold,
The future
Shall ride on a
"Doubled Decker Bus!"

Modern Dilemma

While on a
Zig Zag
Trail
When folks turn
Directionless and
Bit dizzy on the
Way

They're
Lost in the
World of
Misinterpretations
And false narratives

As a
Result
There
Explodes rage
All over and
Sadly killing
Their
Moral Selves...
What a pity!

Bridges
Only

Have
We ever got the
Time to pause and
Think for a change

That all humans
Belong to one another
And together they can
Be formidable force

Have
We ever launched
A large scale meeting
To probe
Such possibilities,
I mean consistently
Or what

Did we ever
Think all humans are
Born equal and good
Why then be obsessed
In building big walls?

Coiled-Spring

Today
An innocent
Child is forced to
Grow up fast and
Asked to swallow
All complexities of
Life so soon

He's asked
To be best in
Everything, anything
But be best of the best
From the very beginning

There ain't time
Left for childhood
I mean,
Happy days to play,
To explore nature and
To build durable
Friendship

What if
The child one day
Decides to runaway and
Become a tranquil Zen
Monk on his own volition!

Subjectivity
Still

It was
A stygian
Night and the storm
Had not gone
But the dead silence
Cascaded the entire
Terrain

Folks began to
Wonder, "what if
They were a
Perennial juveniles
Lost into this corrupt
World or what"

There
Was an eerie
Silence for a while
And one of the elders
Lamented, "what if
We've been on the
Dark side and not
Knowing for a long!"

Another elder added
Rather with a pinch of
Philosophical wisdom,
"What if life has been a
One big riddle and
We're here to untie
The Gordian-knot? "

Never Forget

Listen up
It's a
Zig -Zag trail
All the way 'til
We meet
Truth, truth and
Nothing but the
Truth in the end

A long ways
To go since its
A winding trail at
Every turn, turn
And turn 'til we
Hit the right
Road in the end

Doesn't
Matter how far
The journey's on
Doesn't matter
How long
We got to roll

The trail is
The game of
Truth, the truth and
Nothing
But the truth of
Our souls...

Recent Books by J.J. Bhatt

(From Amazon/Kindle)

HUMAN ENDEAVOR: *Essence & Mission/ a Call for Global Awakening,* (2011)

ROLLING SPIRITS: *Being Becoming /a Trilogy,* (2012)

ODYSSEY OF THE DAMNED: *A Revolving Destiny,* (2013).

PARISHRAM: *Journey of the Human Spirits,* (2014).

TRIUMPH OF THE BOLD: *A Poetic Reality, (2015).*

THEATER OF WISDOM, *(2016).*

MAGNIFICENT QUEST: *Life, Death & Eternity, (2016)*

ESSENCE OF INDIA: *A Comprehensive Perspective, (2016).*

ESSENCE OF CHINA: *Challenges & Possibilities, (2016).*

BEING & MORAL PERSUASION: *A Bolt of Inspiration, (2017).*

REFELCTIONS, RECOLLECTIONS & EXPRESSIONS, (2018).

ONE, TWO, THREE... ETERNITY: *A Poetic Odyssey,* 2018).

INDIA: *Journey of Enlightenment (2019.)*

SPINNING MIND, SPINNING TIME: *C'est la vie (2019). Book 1.*

MEDITATION ON HOLY TRINITY *(2019), Book 2.*

ENLIGHTENMENT: *Fiat lux* (2019), Book 3.

BEING IN THE CONTEXTUAL ORBIT: *Rhythm, Melody & Meaning* (2019)

QUINTESSENCE: *Thought & Action* (2019)

THE WILL TO ASCENT: *Power of Boldness & Genius* (2019)

RIDE ON A SPINNING WHEEL: *Existence Introspected* (2020a)

A FLASH OF LIGHT: *Splendors, Perplexities & Riddles* (2020b)

ON A ZIG ZAG TRAIL: *The Flow of Life* (2020c).

UNBOUNDED: *An Inner Sense of Destiny* (2020d).

JAGDISH J. BHATT, PhD

Brings 45 years of academic experience including
the post-doctorate scientist at Stanford University,
CA. He has authored numerous publications including
28 books which cover the scientific and literary fields.